Nocturnal Nights

Komal Papanwar

BookLeaf Publishing

India | USA | UK

Preface

This collection is born from silence—the kind that echoes
louder than sound.
From moments where voices trembled but didn't break
through,
where truths sat behind smiles,
and where "I'm fine" meant anything but.

These poems are conversations that never happened,
goodbyes that were never given,
and strength that bloomed in secret.
You'll find grief here, and anger.
Softness, survival, and softness again.
They are not always neat.
But neither is healing.

I offer these pages as both mirror and map.
If you've ever felt unheard, unseen, or unnamed—
I hope you find pieces of yourself here.
And I hope you feel less alone.

Acknowledgements

To the quiet resilience of every woman who ever
doubted her voice—thank you for carrying your stories,
even when no one asked for them.

To the poets and truth-tellers who wrote before me,
and the friends who reminded me that my words
mattered:
Your belief made these pages possible.

To the girl I used to be—
I'm sorry I didn't listen sooner.
But I'm here now.
And we're speaking, finally.

1. Two Thirds of Me

These ravenous words,
Threaten to crawl up my throat.
But I express only a third,
And the rest settles in a cryptic note.

It curdles and bubbles,
In the deepest chamber of my heart.
For it has known such troubles,
That it refuses to speak its part.

My skin is set ablaze,
Streams march down my cheek.
I am lost in this twisted maze,
But they mustn't know I'm weak.

And then I am possessed,
By this barbarous brute.
Tearing through my chest,
Reaching for a phantom fruit.

Loud bells reverberate in my ears,
The rage dwells upon my nose.
My thoughts muddle becoming unclear,
The violence I crave, nobody knows.

So it remains unsaid,
Rotting in the pits of my soul.
Fiendish demons it has bred,
Making me two-thirds whole.

2. Verses of Pain

I am well versed,
In the scriptures of pain.
To know it is to be cursed,
By the ghosts of the slain.

Prayers of hollow apologies,
I was taught as a child.
Pray for their disparity,
Of course its worth your while.

The gospels of grief,
And songs of sadness,
Are not a part of our belief,
So I sung them in silence.

You tied my hands,
For the glory of afterlife.
Marched me down *holy* lands,
With my back to your knife.

You chewed me up,
Because I tasted so sweet.
Now I'm a bitter concoction in your cup,
Funny that our eyes won't meet.

You shoved me through hell,
So you could rearrange my shards.
But I am impossible to compel,
I play with my own cards.

So beware of me,
When I say I know pain.
I succumb to no plea,
I can endure it once again.

3. Nature's Play

How I revere,
The beauty of nature's wrath.
How she commands an audience,
When the final straw lands.
They sky is acast,
With a blanket of gloom,
That bleeds into a foreboding hue.
Like a white cloth,
Unanticipatedly turning grey,
At the touch of watery black paint.
The wind cowers,
In the face of her fury.
It scampers hither and thither.
Pushing past leaves and calm waters.
Warning them of what is to come.
Trees clatter and shiver.
Skin of lakes crinkle in worry.
This disturbance in the ether,
Is a brewing a silent cacophony.
Bees zip to their hives.
Toads croak their rhythmic tones.
Birds escape the sky,
And go eerily still in their nests.
A soft static sound penetrates the space.

A pitter for the sadness she could no longer hide.
A patter for the pain she held for so long inside.
A pitter, a patter now vehemently grows,
Into uncontrollable fits of terror.
And Lo! A crescendo!
Her tears like bullets,
Beat relentlessly upon the ground.
The clouds split asunder,
Firing bolts of lightning in revolt.
A thunderous noise ,so great, so terrifying,
Now permeates all corners.
The rivers swell with unbridled rage.
As storms turn the skies into an ominous page.
A spectacle of chaos in wild disarray.
But beauty's essence lingers, its raw ballet.
For even in fury, she holds a grace,
An untamed spirit that time can't erase.

4. If I Were a Man

If I were a man,
I would run amok down the grassy hills,
Paint my clothes with mud,
Without a worry about falling ill.

I would be the king of lands,
With properties stamped in my name.
I would fly to every country,
And surely rise to fame.

Risk would not be a familiar word,
I'd be applauded for my intuition.
"Play it safe"—a term I'd have never heard,
People would call my choice ambition.

I would drive off on a whim,
And come back at 3 AM if I so wished.
I'd sleep beneath a bonfire's glow,
And for once, know what it means to exist.

I would fight with my fists,
And get into bloody brawls.
I would yell at the top of my lungs,
Then walk with pride down the halls.

I would dress the way I wanted,
Without fearing what my mother would say,
And walk the shadiest of streets,
Without casting myself as prey.

I would feed my every impulse,
And that would be okay,
Because that is what a man should do—
I would go unjudged for being that way.

I would howl at the moon,
Study the stars all night.
I'd be left alone if I wished,
Without my thoughts dissected with might.

I would go on adventures,
And write tales about my glory.
I'd battle with dragons,
And people would read my story.

I would be seen as a human
By my mother and father—
Not a burden that needs tending,
A parasite of a daughter.

If I were a man,

I would've known what it means to live,
To taste the fruit of freedom—
There's nothing I wouldn't give.

5. The Cabin

There are days when my mind feels withered,
Thoughts whirling like a frozen tempest, a blizzard.
I yearn for the warm cabin, the refuge deep in the pines,
Where silence wraps around me and solitude aligns.

I trudge through the weight of the day,
Like wading through snow that won't melt away.
My footsteps vanish beneath the fallen snow,
The battles I've fought, only my scars will know.

The winter wind screeches and howls with all might,
But my heart is set on the soft glow of the cabin's light.
I crumble at the doorstep, crying with a strange, sweet relief,
The cabin groans in stillness, echoing my long felt grief.

I shed the doubts like a heavy coat at the door,
I kick my insecurities like muddy boots on the floor.
I disrobe all judgement, one layer at a time,
I cloak myself in kindness that always should've been mine.

The crackle of the hearth mutes the storm outside,
Its radiating warmth thaws my soul from the inside.

I stir my teacup, watching my thoughts dissolve,
I sip from it gently, and smile at the distant resolve.

The plush billowy blankets invite me to its embrace,
I gladly answer its call and glide towards it with no
haste.
I let the snow gather at the door and let it seal me in,
For the eternal slumber I so longed for is about to begin.

6. Words That Don't Reach

There are hurricanes in my head,
A stew of thoughts in my brain.
Secretive codes in the tears I shed
Unsaid words my heart does retain.

I am entwirled in a veil,
That only I can see.
You think I am of no avail,
But how I long to be free.

Every word that launches from my mouth,
Every song i sing or solemn ode I cry.
Disintegrates upon reaching that shroud,
You just can't see how much I try.

There are oceans between us,
So I scream with all rigor.
But who cares? nobody does,
They're all on the shore.

Every syllable I enunciate,
Plunges straight into the water.
Down at the depths they stagnate,
Carcasses of the slaughter.

The warped enigmatic monsters,
That lurk in the abyss.
Nourish off the shards of martyrs,
Perhaps a distant memory they reminisce.

On these remnants they grow,
Into wild wild behemoths.
But these miscreations know,
The words I long to breathe.

So these leviathans thrive,
And drown me in my poems.
Into their depths I dive,
And rule the haunted waters.

7. My Soul knows

I have lost my soul,
Deep in the misty woods.
And there she lies complete and whole,
Being true to the dreams of my childhood.
She rests at the snow capped mountain top,
Howling with the wolves under that luminous, round
moon.
Galloping with the winter winds, her hair untamed,
Racing towards her destiny with a grit so true.

Follow her! I tell myself

But she fades into the veils of the night,
No path unfolds, no stars align.
My soul, My soul, how I yearn for her light!
In this darkness, I have lost what was mine.

Yet the echoes of laughter twirl through the night,
A whisper of courage calls me to fight.
The shadows may stretch, but I will not cower,
With each weary step, I reclaim my power.

Through thickets and thorns, I tread with resolve,
For the heart's silent yearning, I must solve.

With a flicker of hope igniting my core,
I will search for her essence, forevermore.

8. Crazy

If I was a child of five, so sweet and small,
And I told you I wanted to touch the sky.
You would tell me to grow strong and tall,
And they'll brush past my cheeks as they pass by.

So I filled my head with bursting ideas,
And my heart pumped on the beat of passion.
Daydreams of my future filled me with euphoria,
With all excitement, I was ready to jump into action.

I wore my pride like a paper crown,
I drew stars with rainbow crayons on every wall.
I knew that the world would never let me down,
If I kept my chin up and listened to the nature's call.

But time whispered doubts with a colder tone,
The sky I chased seemed farther away.
And slowly, I felt more lost than grown,
Clouded in the smog of each passing day.

I'd tell you my ambitions and dreams,
Hoping you would re-ignite my spark.
But you look at me like a hollowed out machine,
Label me crazy and walk past me with a snark.

You belittled me for wanting so much more,
You bleach my thoughts with reality.
With my mind in chaos, head straight to the door,
To my forgotten dreamland I flee.

All I yearned was buried beneath the dirt,
Unearthing the colors you made me fold.
It hardened with years of silence and hurt,
But I will dig with hands both bare and bold.

9. Candle

Sweet and slender,
Her mesmerizing glow.
The flame a gentle dancer,
Swaying to and fro.

She bobs with elegance,
By the windowsill frame.
She marks her eminence,
In twilight hours' acclaim.

She dances without sound,
But the rhythm of her mind.
Her radiance flowing unbound,
A moment long enshrined.

She draws the room in hush,
A tender, watchful gleam.
Her light—a gentle blush,
That drifts between a dream.

In shadows softly cast,
Her whispers weave through air,
A tale of moments past,
Of secrets held with care.

As she burns through the hours,
The wax seeps down her spine.
Her body thins and bows,
Nearing the end of her time.

As dawn begins to break,
Her glow withdraws and wanes.
Yet in her silent wake,
The echo still remains.

10. Change

Why did she change?
Why did she go away?
Why couldn't she engage,
In a conversation for just one more day?

She loved me like her dearest sheep,
And I gave her all my wool.
But she butchered me in my sleep,
When the moon wasn't even full.

I sharpened her swords,
When we played knights.
But she stabbed me, not with her words,
But with what she didn't make right.

And when I raged,
I raged with might.
But her expression remained caged,
Nothing reached that night.

So I locked the doors of my heart,
And threw the key away.
In the deep cellar it won't contort,
And there it will stay.

11. Walls

I built these walls around my heart,
To keep me safe from the very start.
Through pain and grit I hammered them tight,
Trapped in my cage, I set myself alight.

I burned and burned, but did not make a sound,
For I coughed and choked on this reticence newfound.
The smoldering embers lapped at my skin,
And like and old friend, I let them in.

The vines grew thick and swallowed my fort,
Slow and steady, my days began to grow short.
The ramparts, they held, ever so strong.
No hurt could pass, no voice, no wrong.

So in my prison I sit and dwell on my thoughts,
While the barrage from the world goes on and on.
Ash coats the stone where my battles were fought,
And the fire I fed now flickers—withdrawn.

My breath is a ghost that drifts through the stone,
I carved out a kingdom to suffer alone.
Let the world rage, I no longer fight,
For I am the dark, and I've snuffed out the light.

No key fits the lock I forged in my youth,
No flame can reveal what I buried in truth.
I traded the world for a whispering wall,
And now I watch shadows that never will fall.

12. Writing

I thought about writing,
Something meaningful and true.
But I couldn't find the right words,
To convey what I meant to you.

I scribbled out my thoughts,
Read it over and over again.
I circled some of the words,
And continued to wrack my brain.

I stirred the thoughts that wouldn't set—
A brew of doubt and flame.
Each sentence swam, then quickly fled,
Too wild for me to name.

I reached for one, it slipped away—
A ghost behind my eyes.
The more I tried to pin it down,
The more it wore disguise.

I crumpled drafts like fallen leaves,
Their ink too faint, or far too loud.
My silence filled the space between,
What I could say and what's allowed.

I watched the pages pile and sigh,
A forest at my feet.
Each failure bore a trace of truth,
That made the silence sweet.

The page, once blank, now bears the scars,
Of every single attempt.
Each mark a thought I couldn't shape,
Each smudge a feeling kept.

So here's this page—half-formed, unsure—
Still missing what I meant to say.
But maybe you'll read between the lines,
And find my heart tucked in the grey.

13. Safe House

I built a house beyond the trees,
In the quiet hush of the fallen leaves.
It overlooked the ocean's cry,
But stayed untouched beneath the sky.

The woods grew thick to guard my gate,
A winding path I let time make.
No roads were drawn, no signs were placed,
Only the wind could know this face.

Its walls were made of things I kept—
Of poems wept and secrets slept.
The hearth burned low with gentle grace,
A warmth I made, a sacred place.

The floors are worn from where I pace,
Each corner holds a known embrace.
The windows hum with ocean air,
Salt-kissed and sweet beyond compare.

I run there when the world feels loud,
When thoughts press in, a heavy cloud.
Its walls don't ask the reasons why,
They hold me close and let me cry.

But you would seek it, torch in hand,
With questions sharp you'd stalk the land.
You'd tear through brush and force the door,
To peer inside and search for more.

You'd strip the paint to read the grain,
Then wonder why I don't explain.
And when you left, the floorboards cried,
My shelter gone, my heart outside.

14. A Home Survival Guide

One:
Smile when they ask what's on your mind,
But make sure your truth is safely confined.
Pick from the choices they prepare,
And nod like freedom's really there.

Two:
Never offer your opinion,
Especially when it is asked.
This home is their dominion,
Your words must remain masked.

Three:
Always be polite,
And be humble when you speak.
If they demean you will all might,
Happily accept their critique.

Four:
Do not try to cross them,
At least not in broad daylight.
When confronted, play dumb.
Your true self belongs to the night.

Five:
Wear your joy like your favorite shirt—
Pressed, uncreased, and bright.
God forbid you show your hurt,
Your pain must stay out of sight.

Six:
They are always right,
And you are always wrong.
Never ever put up a fight,
Humor them and play along.

Seven:
Paint your face with a gleam so wide,
Mask the lines beneath your skin.
Every crack you try to hide,
Should vanish deep within.

Eight:
Eat what they give you,
And swallow their lies.
Inhale their special brew,
Its really their anger in disguise.

Nine:
You may go where you wish,
As long as you don't stray too far.

They'll lock you up in a swish,
If you don't tell where you are.

Ten:
Friends are not required,
Family is all you need.
Friends will leave you when they're tired,
Family will hold you till you bleed.

Eleven:
Follow these rules will all your heart,
And you'll be their perfect guest.
As long as you abide to your part,
You'll be safely trapped in their nest.

15. Conversation Between the Moon and a Street Lamp

The moon peeked out from a curtain of cloud,
Soft in her glow, serene and proud.
She looked down at the streetlamp's light,
Flickering gold in the hush of the night.

"You burn too bright," the moon began
"Always buzzing like a broken fan.
Do you ever rest, or ever dream?
You stain the dark with your harsh gleam."

The streetlamp blinked, then gave a sigh,
"I dream of silence beneath the sky.
But people fear the dark, you see—
So I stand and shine out endlessly."

"You mimic me," the moon replied,
"But lack the pull, the shifting tide.
I change with moods, with storms and seas—
You only hum for passerby's."

"I may not move," the lamp confessed,
"But I guard children on their quest.
I catch the keys, the lovers' glance,

The fox that slips by in a midnight dance."

The moon grew quiet, a little dim,
Touched by something deep within.
Then softly said, "Perhaps you're right—
There's room for all that brings us light."

So they stood in mutual grace that hour,
The moon, aloof with silver power,
And the streetlamp, humble in his beam,
Both keepers of someone's quiet dream.

16. For a Star That's Tired of Shining

Hey.

You there.

Yes, you—the one burning at both ends of infinity.

The one holding galaxies on your shoulders like it's just another Tuesday.

You don't have to shine tonight.

Breathe.

Take in the silence between pulses.

Even stars have heartbeats,

and you've skipped yours for centuries—

pouring out light like love letters

to a sky that never writes back.

Let your edges flicker.

Let the glow go soft.

This is not weakness.

This…

is rhythm.

Remember:

You are not a god.

Not every spark needs to be seen.

Not every orbit needs your gravity.

Let them whisper,
Let them wonder,
Let them say,
"I think that one used to shine brighter."
Good.
Let them miss you.

Dim gently.
No need for theatrics.
You don't have to supernova just to prove you were here.
Some stars bow out without fanfare,
folding into the arms of the cosmos
like the last note of a lullaby.
Be the hush
after the thunder.
The calm
after the blaze.

If you must, send one last flare.
A subtle goodbye.
A shimmer caught in the eye of a child
peering through a telescope
thinking it's magic.
Maybe it is.
Maybe that's enough.

Fall inward.

Not down.
Not away.
Inward.
It's not collapse.
It's return.
To stillness.
To self.
To that singular point you began from
before time gave you a name.
The universe does not mourn
its exhausted stars—
it repurposes them.
You are becoming
the soil of future light.

Sleep.
You've burned enough.
Fought enough.
Given enough.
You've lit the path for travelers,
warmed cold moons,
made wishes possible.
Now—
let the dark cradle you
like the ancient thing you are.
Lie back in the fabric of space
and just...

be.
You do not need to shine
to be a star.

17. I Met My Past Self at a Bus Stop

I met my past self at a stop one night,
Under flickering glow and pale streetlight.
She swung her legs and hummed a tune,
A crooked smile beneath the moon.

She looked about ten, maybe barely nine,
Shoelaces tied, hair in line.
Clutching a notebook, pages worn,
Filled with dreams both wild and torn.

"You're late," she said with narrowed eyes,
"Have you learned to reach the skies?
Do we become an astronaut?
Or did we lose the spark we brought?"

I laughed and sat there by her side,
Brushed the wind and checked my pride.
"Not quite the stars," I softly said,
"But dreams, you see, they shift instead."

Her eyes grew wide—"Do we still draw?
Still build things just to drop a jaw?
Do we sing songs that no one hears?

Do we still write away our fears?"

I bit my lip and took a breath,
Thinking of silence loud as death.
"Some things we lose, some things we hide,
But some come back when pain subsides."

She frowned a bit and kicked the ground,
Unspoken words still whirling round.
"Do we still cry when no one's near?
Do we still hide when faced with fear?"

I met her gaze, so sharp, so clear—
"Sometimes, yes. But less each year.
We've learned that breaking doesn't mean
We're any less than what we've been."

The bus rolled in with tired groans,
A ghostly sound of engine tones.
She stood but paused before the door,
"Will we become the kid who swore—

That she would never trade his soul,
For comfort, silence, or control?"
I looked at her, and took her hand,
"That kid still fights to help us stand."

She boarded then, with one last grin,
A younger voice beneath my skin.
And though she left without a name,
I walked away, somehow the same.

18. The Secret Life of Socks

They vanish it seems, without a trace—
One from the pair, gone into space.
No hole, no tear, no parting note—
Just emptiness where they once did float.

But listen closely, late at night,
When the laundry room dims its final light—
You'll hear them whisper, soft and low,
Plotting the places they long to go.

Left socks are dreamers, wild and bold,
They slip through cracks when the dryer gets cold.
Right socks are loyal, they stay behind—
Guarding the drawer, silently resigned.

One's in Paris, beneath a shoe,
Learning to tango in red and blue.
Another hitchhikes through Japan,
Knotted like a bandana 'round a traveler's hand.

One's a puppet in a kids' backyard play,
Preaching justice in a woolly way.
One's been stitched into a patchwork quilt
With stories of freedom and no dryer guilt.

There's a sock who writes memoirs
In an attic somewhere,
Titled: *"Threadbare But Free:*
My Journey Through Air."

They meet once a year
In a lost-and-found drawer
To toast to the ones
Who are lost no more.

So next time you curse
That mysterious fate
That leaves one sock standing
Without its mate—

Just know it's not lost,
Nor gone to waste—
It's off living life
At its own sockish pace.

19. Museum of Things That Never Happened

Welcome, dear dreamer, step through the gate,
To halls of what-ifs, too early or late.
Where silence is hung in elaborate frames,
And each empty space whispers forgotten names.

Here's the letter you never wrote,
Sealed in a bottle that stayed afloat.
It drifts on display in a sea of glass,
Next to the call you didn't make last.

A photograph glows in sepia blur—
You, beside someone you never were.
You're laughing, clearly, in mid-spin flight,
With the stranger you almost loved that night.

Down this corridor—past the velvet rope—
Is The Room of Every Derailed Hope.
College applications never sent,
Journals stopped mid-sentence, pages bent.

There's a dusty podium, clean and grand,
Where you never took the promised stand.
A trophy shines with a name not yours,

Next to a stage with unopened doors.

Look—
The Gallery of Almosts gleams dim but wide,
With blueprints of dreams you buried inside.
An instrument you never learned to play
Cries notes in the echoes of things you'd say.

There's a wing for loves that flickered, then fell—
Flickering still in glass carousel.
Each one spins slowly, fragile and bright,
Glowing faint in the low museum light.

And just when the loss becomes too tight,
There's a bench in the corner—soft, and white.
A place for the guests to quietly grieve
The selves they imagined but couldn't retrieve.

But before you go, one final view:
A blank frame reserved for future you.
Still unwritten. Still unknown.
Still free to escape this vaulted zone.

Because sometimes the things
that never came true
are reminders
of what you still can do.

20. The Archive of Lost Dreams

There's a room where no light dares to fall,
A place where silence is the loudest call.
Walls lined with dust and forgotten schemes,
A quiet archive of lost dreams.

In this vault, they sleep, one by one—
Dreams that withered before they'd begun,
Unspoken wishes, promises bent,
Plans that faded with time's descent.

The dream of the painter, brushes untouched,
The writer whose words never felt much.
The pilot who longed to take flight,
But stayed grounded, too scared of the height.

There's a shelf for the books that never were read,
A drawer for the life you almost led.
A folder of songs that nobody heard,
Unwritten, unfinished, without a word.

The clock ticks on with no hands to show—
How long, how far those dreams let go.
Some are tattered, some are pristine,

All with a story that might have been.

A note from the lover who didn't dare speak,
The traveler whose path grew far too weak.
The artist who feared their colors would fade,
The scientist whose theories never were made.

But still, they wait, in soft refrain,
Hoping one day to rise again.
For the archive, though vast and deep,
Holds treasures it doesn't wish to keep.

Every dream has a place, in silence to rest,
Not forgotten, but waiting, in the chest.
For when the heart is ready to try,
And the mind's open wings are willing to fly.

So here's to the dreams that slip away,
That rest in the archive, where shadows play.
One day they may find the spark they need,
To rise again and finally succeed.

21. Zoning Out

I sit, but I'm not here,
Just a body lost in the blur of air,
Eyes fixed on something, or nothing at all,
A drift, a float, a quiet fall.

The words around me pulse and hum,
Like distant waves, they're barely sung.
I nod, I smile, but inside,
I'm somewhere else, nowhere to hide.

Thoughts scatter like autumn leaves,
Twirling, tumbling, then they freeze.
I try to catch one, but it slips away,
A fleeting moment, a brief delay.

Time stretches like a rubber band,
A second long, a minute grand.
I'm caught between the world outside,
And the ocean of thoughts where I reside.

The sound of my name feels far away,
As if spoken in another day.
I blink, I breathe, I nod again,
But my mind is off in places unclaimed.

A door in my mind creaks open wide,
I step through it, no need to decide.
Past the clutter, past the noise,
I find peace in the quiet void.

And then—
A snap, a click, I'm back again,
The world returns, the voices blend.
But just for a moment, I slip away—
A brief vacation, before the fray.

Zoning out, I've learned to do,
A little retreat, a silent hue.
Where thoughts can wander, calm and free,
In the space between you and me.

22. Letting Go

I held on like the tide holds shore,
Clinging to what was, not what's in store.
Afraid that loosening meant I'd lose
The part of me I didn't choose.

I cupped the past in trembling hands,
Its brittle weight like desert sands.
But fingers tire and hearts grow still
When pressed too long against the will.

So I uncurled, slow and unsure,
Let silence slip in through the door.
I named the grief, I faced the ache,
And learned that peace is what we make.

Not in the fixing, not the fight—
But in surrendering to the night.
Where broken things can gently rest,
And healing finds an open chest.

I left behind what wasn't mine,
Old dreams that soured over time.
And in their place, a softer hue—
The dawn of something calm and true.

Not every ending needs a flame,
Not every ghost deserves a name.
Some stories close like whispered prayer,
And peace walks in through thinner air.

So now I float, not out of fear,
But knowing I was never near
To losing what I truly own—
The self that flowers when alone.